WORDS AND THE WORD

CHRISTOPHER DERRICK

WORDS AND THE WORD

Notes on Our Catholic Vocabulary

IGNATIUS PRESS   SAN FRANCISCO

Cover by Victoria Hoke Lane

With ecclesiastical approval
© 1987 Ignatius Press, San Francisco
All rights reserved
ISBN 0-89870-130-9
Library of Congress catalogue number 86-62926
Printed in the United States of America

INTRODUCTION

Language is a sacred thing. *Logos* or utterance or meaning or 'Word' is among the names of God, and it refers to something almost sacramental. *Efficit quod significat*: within the hearer's mind, any word effects what it also signifies. So language needs reverential handling—not always, since there's plenty of lawful scope for linguistic fun, but in serious matters most certainly.

It needs effective handling as well, and especially by us Catholics, since a huge proportion of the Church's apostolic and pastoral work is necessarily linguistic or verbal and will fail where language is handled badly. We are people with a message, something to enact but also something to *say*: we operate in the field now called 'communication', we're in the word-industry. And if you operate in some industry, you need to understand your tools first of all, and then keep them polished and sharp and in good working order generally.

This book stems from a conviction that the Church's verbal tool-kit, while far from being in total disrepair, displays signs of inattention and neglect at many key points; also, that our task of 'communication'—both internal and external—is thereby made needlessly difficult. We aren't accomplishing it so very successfully, which isn't entirely our own fault: we were warned from the start that much of the seed would fall on stony ground, that many people would lack "ears to hear". But that doesn't justify us in doing anything short of our best.

The problem, as encountered by myself over many years as a Catholic writer and controversialist, is mostly a matter of semantic change and semantic complexity.

Now I fully expect that statement of the case to arouse a certain distrust. There are still some Catholics who talk as though every word possessed its own single, unambiguous, objective, and changeless 'meaning', put into it at the dawn of time by God or Adam or Plato, so that any other use of it becomes a simple malapropism or mistake. Anyone who questions this grossly unhistorical idea will be suspected—in some quarters—of proposing a kind of conceptual and verbal relativism and so of undermining all logic and indeed all faith.

By way of a general reply to such people, I offer

a bashful suggestion that, since the Middle Ages, various things may conceivably have been discovered—or *noticed*—about what language is and how it works.

In particular, I suggest that it is inattention to language, and to ambiguity in particular, which really does put logic at risk. Writing about scholasticism in its late-mediaeval decline, a writer whose name I forget once said something like this: "They seem to have thought that words were perfectly rigid structures, which only needed to be bolted together according to the known rules of the syllogism in order to reach any height and support any weight." But in their natural habitat—common usage—words seldom have that monolithic and rigid quality. We look for a single meaning, and we commonly find only a loose and shifting cluster of associated meanings: the consequent ambiguity endangers the rigour of any single syllogism, so enabling a chain of consecutive syllogisms to go wildly astray.

We avoid this danger, of course, in so far as we achieve perfect precision in defining our terms—that is, in giving each one a specialised *ad hoc* sense, far narrower than it carries in common usage. But semantic complexity is what makes that into a necessary prelude to all logical discourse, and semantic change is conspicuous among the responsible factors. No Catholic has any need to distrust either concept.

My point is that if we seek to practise and promote the Church's work of communication, we cannot prudently ignore the tools which we handle, the medium in which we operate. A preoccupation with higher things may tempt us to do so. But as I have observed, language is an exceedingly high thing in itself.

So we should pay habitually close attention to words and meanings; and within 'meanings', emotional and imaginative overtones must definitely be included. In the name of pure logic, we may possibly try to exclude them from our own utterances. But they are more than likely to affect what gets across *ad modum recipientium*.

And all the time, we should remember that we are dealing with at least three separate languages, more or less distinct but tending to overlap and shade off into one another, so making for confusion. There's our own Catholic language, once fairly precise but now—thanks mostly to postconciliar trauma—suffering various internal ambiguities and tensions. Then there's the looser semi-religious language of the vaguely post-Christian people around us; and then, affecting the other two, there's the wholly secularised language of a predominantly sceptical and positivistic culture. One practical difficulty is that this last is hardly more capable of carrying sacred meanings than the language of a primitive Stone-Age tribe would be capable of carrying electronic meanings.

Such problems should be our daily concern, if we desire to preach the eternal Word by means of our own temporal words.

So I offer this book as one man's attempt to "purify the dialect of the tribe", or at least to suggest—by illustration rather than analysis—certain senses in which that purification is needed, certain lines along which it might proceed. A short book, and it is neither definitive nor exhaustive: the reader will find points of disagreement and inexplicable omissions as well. I shall welcome his criticisms and suggestions. If accepted, they will entitle him to a free copy of any second edition.

AUTHORITY

This word has two quite different meanings in modern English, and the difference between them is of some importance to Catholics.

In one sense, 'authority' is a right to be obeyed, or a power to compel obedience, or both. We thus speak of 'the public authorities'; and in an army or anything like it, authority of this disciplinary kind plays a crucial part. Something of the same sort—however gently exercised—is necessary in practically every group activity of human beings, and it is rooted in the animal side of our nature: various patterns of 'dominance and submission' are to be observed among the beasts.

Our responses to this kind of authority can of course vary. Where personal liberty is made into an absolute—as it so widely is today—it can be seen as outrageous in itself, as can any suggestion that we might need to obey. We may need to remember that *Non serviam*—"I refuse to obey!"—was always the motto of Hell. At the other extreme, there can be such a thing as pathological docility. Some people are so very timid that they cannot bear to act, or even to think, except in obedience to authoritative commands from somebody else.

That's one kind of 'authority'. But when we say that a great scholar is an 'authority' on his subject, we don't mean that he issues commands in connection with it: we only mean that he knows what he's talking about. He isn't infallible, but we can treat him as a fairly reliable guide to that subject, though possibly not to anything else.

The difference is substantial. The first kind of authority speaks in the imperative and calls for obedience; the second kind speaks in the indicative and (we hope) deserves assent.

Both kinds are found in the Church—the first kind because it is (among other things) a group activity of human beings, and the second because it speaks with the voice of Christ and therefore knows what it's talking about. Ecclesiastical discipline is a necessary thing, despite the obvious dangers, and that kind of authority hardly impinges at all upon the layman: inner and outer assent to the teaching authority of the Church is a totally different thing and very much more important for all of us.

The two are often confused in anti-Catholic writing, and sometimes (I fear) deliberately. Ever since Newman's *Apologia*, we have seen a steady stream of conversion-narratives, autobiographical accounts of how each enquirer found his way, not unaided, into the one true Fold of the Redeemer; and in many such books, the enquiry is seen in terms of a search for 'authority' in religion. That gives the hostile commentator his chance. "Exactly! These Catholics, their converts especially, are a bunch of pathologically timid weaklings, father-fixated and irresolute, seeking above all else to be *ordered around*. That's the great attraction of the papacy. As his title shows, the Pope acts as a Daddy-surrogate, comforting people by giving them clear-cut marching-orders. But a mature adult shouldn't need anything of that sort."

It's extremely foolish to offer psychological explanations of any discovery or retention of Catholic faith, since Catholics—converts included—are wildly diverse people and of every conceivable type, psychologically speaking. That diagnosis of the convert's motivations may conceivably be accurate in isolated cases. But in the vast majority, it isn't a matter of "Who will satisfy my longing to be bossed around and given orders?", but of "In these matters, is there anyone who really knows what he's talking about?" That's a very different thing.

When we read that the Lord spoke "with authority" and not like the Scribes and Pharisees, we should probably understand the word in both senses. He commanded: he also *knew*.

CATHOLIC

In common usage, this word means 'Roman Catholic'. It has certain other senses, but I do not propose to consider them here.

But even in that dominant sense, it is far from being unambiguous. The expression "I am a Catholic" can be intended to carry three distinct meanings at least.

Surprisingly often, we find it used as a simple assertion of family or ethnic identity. It then means "I come of Catholic stock and am not prepared to make a formal break with our own people." The speaker has no intention of conveying *religious* information about himself: his belief and practice may be anything or nothing.

Then, we find that same expression used in a clearly religious sense but with a qualification which is sometimes implied and sometimes spelled out: "I am a Catholic, of course, but. . . ." If pressed, the speaker will often invoke such terms as 'liberal' or 'progressive' or even 'postconciliar' (see COUNCIL) by way of explaining that qualification. Such terms mean that while he claims the Catholic name, he does not give the 'assent of faith' to the actual teachings of the Church: he gives them the selective assent of his critical judgment, and that's a very different thing. We might there speak of a 'selective Catholic', and with ironic awareness of the contradiction there implied (see HERESY).

Such people present us with a curious problem in psychology and motivation. A fervently believing Communist will often (and sensibly) see through that delusory faith, what with greater wisdom or bitter experience or both: he will very seldom continue to describe himself as a Communist, even in some Pickwickian sense of his own. But it's no rare thing to meet someone whose mind has moved miles and miles away from anything remotely like 'the mind of the Church', but who still insists on calling himself a Catholic. If you challenge his right to that title— not necessarily for the sake of religious orthodoxy, but perhaps for the sake of verbal clarity alone—he will usually become extremely angry. He wants the word 'Catholic' to have acquired infinite elasticity of meaning: he doesn't want to face the fact that it would then have no effective meaning at all.

In this confused and indeed contradictory sense, the word is often applied to schools and colleges and periodicals and much else, not only to individuals.

Finally, there's the obvious sense in which the expression "I am a Catholic" can be taken at its face value. It then implies no claim to sanctity; but it does imply—among many other things—a habitual willingness to give the 'assent of faith' wherever the Church calls for exactly that. In the concrete, ignorance or misunderstanding can sometimes frustrate the implementation of that willingness. But it has to be there. It's one central element in what 'a Catholic' means when coherently said.

Its great enemy is the proud spirit of "I (or We) know better." You don't.

CELEBRATION

This word has recently acquired a new and semi-facetious sense, unrelated to anything in its long history. In this new sense, it is sometimes invoked in order to justify liturgical aberrations of a decidedly questionable sort.

The argument goes something like this. "The Mass is a celebration: the officiating priest has long been described as the 'celebrant'. So why can't it be more *like* a celebration? Why should it be a gloomy affair of long faces and hushed voices? David danced before the Ark: why shouldn't we dance at Mass? Why shouldn't we shake the building with our loud bellowings, as anciently recommended in the *Exsultet*? Let's liven things up, let's have fun, let's really *celebrate!*"

What then? Brightly coloured toy balloons? People hugging and kissing one another, or clowning in clown's dress? Topless nuns, perhaps, singing *The Red Flag* under strobe lights? I don't know how far it has gone, and I don't intend to find out.

The argument is not altogether a bad one. The ancient temple worship of Israel, from which our liturgy partly descends, was—by modern English standards at least—a loud tumultuous affair, smoky and no doubt smelly, a 'celebration' that we might well have deemed riotous. Even today, an Englishman can be somewhat astonished by the Dionysiac or Corybantic element in the Catholic worship of Mediterranean countries, among the poor especially. Are we too refined?

A good question. I'd feel happier about these current versions of liturgical 'celebration', however, if they sprang naturally and unselfconsciously from the ordinary life and instincts of poor people in some ancient and deeply religious culture. Among ourselves, they strike me as being *contrived*, theoretically worked out by clever people as an assertion—one among many—of discontinuity with the Catholic past. To me at least, they ring false.

You may disagree; but at least, let us not be deceived by words.

When we look into the past of 'celebration' and cognate words, we start off with the idea of something frequented, then of something that happens often, then of some public observance, then of proclamation: a 'celebrated' man is one whose name has gone out to the whole earth. We're thinking of some great occasion, some grand assertion.

Now when there's a great occasion, we sometimes have a drink: more than one, perhaps, or even too many.

Hence the new and highly specialised sense of the word. "Charlie appears to have been celebrating", we say, as he staggers out of the bar in our direction. Or, on receiving good news: "This calls for a celebration!", and we pop the champagne.

It's hard to use the word nowadays without having some suggestion of a more or less riotous party somewhere at the back of one's mind. But nothing of remotely that sort was implied when we started to call the officiating priest a 'celebrant'. His was simply a public observance, a proclamation.

Liturgically speaking, is there no point of balance between gloom and riotousness?

One difficulty is that the word 'solemn' has become enormously weakened: it has come to suggest only gloom, or at least a careful abstention from visible delight. Let there be no foolish laughter on this solemn occasion!

But a happy child at play never laughs: he never even smiles. He is taken up totally and most seriously into what he's doing; which doesn't mean that he's gloomy. He's blissful, and utterly solemn in consequence.

He could provide us with a good model for our liturgical solemnities or celebrations. Those who would like to take that possibility further are referred to *A Preface to Paradise Lost* by C. S. Lewis, chapter three.

CHRISTIANITY
(and CHRISTIAN)

Semantically speaking, these two words are in very poor shape. In the absence of careful explanation, their use is likely to promote confusion rather than communication.

For the purposes of the dictionary, 'Christianity' is a catch-all term: it indicates all religion that attaches a uniquely central and crucial importance to Jesus of Nazareth. Such religion can of course be a matter of total dedication at one extreme and of a perfunctory and barely remembered loyalty at the other. "I'm a Christian" can sometimes mean "It's the church that I don't go to, not the synagogue or the mosque."

Beyond that, the *content* of 'Christianity' is extremely vague. Even where commitment is serious, it covers so wide a variety in belief, in morality, in worship and organisation and activity, as to make it a blunt instrument indeed for purposes of communication. There is that nominal centrality of

CHRISTIANITY (AND CHRISTIAN) 23

Jesus. But if we try to sharpen the word by doctrinal and other stipulations—by insisting, say, that 'Christianity' only deserves the name where it includes full belief in Incarnation and Resurrection and Atonement—we shall be departing from most common usage. There will then be confusion unless we explain ourselves; and if we do, we shall probably be called 'sectarian' and 'dogmatic'.

In most common usage, however, the word does include one curiously dogmatic implication. "I'm a Christian, of course, but I haven't much use for the Churches" or "for organised religion". Such things are often said; and the implication is that while unspecified 'Christianity' is a noble ideal and a good thing generally, it is betrayed rather than promoted by 'the Churches'. Alternatively and rather more favourably, they are often seen as standing to 'Christianity' as parts to a whole, or as particulars to a universal. Those who take such a view will usually suppose themselves to be transcending all 'denominational' differences: in fact, they will be taking a strictly Protestant ecclesiology for granted.

Further difficulties arise from the fact that over wide areas of popular use, each of these two words has practically ceased to be a religiously descriptive term and has become an ethically evaluative term instead. In a great many contexts, the effective meaning of 'Christianity' is 'altruism', its antonym being something like 'selfishness'.

We already have those ethical words, and we hardly need synonyms for them—certainly not if, by implication, they attribute habitual selfishness to Jews and Hindus and Moslems and the rest.

Given their present semantic condition, I suggest that these two words are best avoided, though 'Christianity' does retain some usefulness as a term of *cultural* classification. It's in that sense alone that I can claim to be living in a 'Christian' country. That was also the sense that was once invoked, in my presence, by an Italian waiter. I was having lunch in Rome, and a saffron-robed group of Hare Krishna devotees shuffled past the window, clapping their hands and ringing their little bells. The waiter looked upon them with contempt. "*Non sono Cristiani*", he said, they aren't Christians.

I don't suppose that his contempt was deeply theological. They weren't people like us: that was their great offence.

CHURCH

'A building used for Christian worship': we have no problem there, or in the necessary distinctions from 'chapel' and 'cathedral' (but see CHRISTIAN). When less architecturally used, however, this is a decidedly complex word. Within the Catholic vocabulary alone, it is used in several different ways.

a. *Theologically* while also *historically*. In this primary sense, we speak of *the* Church, One and Holy and Catholic and Apostolic. This is a continuing mode of the Incarnation, divine but human as well: she's the Body of Christ, his presence and operation in this world, and she's also—inextricably—a human and historical institution, within which human imperfections must always be visible. Mistakes of both the quasi-Arian and the quasi-Docetist kind can therefore be made about her.

In this primary sense, the word is incapable of going into the plural.

b. *Geographically*. In the New Testament, we find mention of 'the Churches'. These may be defined as local incarnations of the One Church in this place or that place: each was what would later be called a diocese or patriarchate. But what with the migration of various peoples, the word (in this sense) is less simply geographical than it was: it can now have ethnic or cultural reference, as when we find Ukrainian Catholics living in the United States and having their own 'Church' there, as well as their own churches.

This plural usage has always been acceptable to the Catholic mind. A Cardinal, as such, is *Sanctae Romanae Ecclesiae Presbyter Cardinalis*, a notably important priest of the 'Church' or—precisely—the Diocese of Rome, whatever position he may hold elsewhere. We also speak without unease of the Uniate 'Churches', though some might there prefer the word 'rite', which has a long association with the geographical term 'patriarchate'. None the less, many Catholics feel reluctant to speak of 'the Churches' in the plural: in the absence of careful explanation, the word can then seem to carry its denominational sense (see below).

c. *Functionally*. A common figure of speech allows us to use the name of a whole when referring to a specifically functioning part. Those who write about international politics, for example, speak quite naturally as though the acts of a government were acts of its entire country: France did this, Germany did that. This convention is taken for granted and bothers nobody; and it shouldn't bother anybody when the acts of a Pope or Council are attributed to 'the Church'.

The use of 'Church' to mean 'clergy' is common among Anglicans but (I think) rare among Catholics.

d. *Denominationally*. It is not linguistically absurd to speak of 'the Churches' with reference to those numerous institutions and bodies of opinion which claim the CHRISTIAN name but are in total separation from Catholic unity. But this usage presupposes a decidedly un-Catholic ecclesiology while also inviting confusion with (b), above. In that connection, the Second Vatican Council therefore preferred to speak of 'ecclesial bodies'—a clumsy term, but tactically useful at a time when ECUMENISM has made HERESY and SCHISM into dirty words, not to be used in polite company. Until we can overcome that prudery, we would benefit from some new term, less clumsy but carrying that same sense as inoffensively as possible. Will somebody please invent it?

For controversial reasons, some people like to say 'the Church of Rome' with reference to the Universal and Petrine Church. This usage should always be challenged, since it generates confusion between these various senses of a complex word.

COLLEGIALITY

Some of us need to remember that the sacrament of Holy Orders exists in three grades alone: Deacon, Priest and Bishop. There isn't a further grade of Pope, or even of Cardinal or Archbishop. To forget this is to incur some risk of exaggerated ULTRAMONTANISM or papolatry, as though the Church were meant to be run as an absolute dictatorship.

When carefully used, the word 'collegiality' can serve as a useful reminder in that sense. It comes, of course, from 'college'—a word which, in its distant origins, meant no more than 'corporate body', with no necessary reference to education. (The same is true of 'university'.) The point is that the Lord conferred the apostolic and episcopal function upon a specific corporate body which by no means included all or most of his believing followers. It's also true to say that within this apostolic college—not exactly *above* it—Saint Peter and his successors were to have a crucial primacy and a particular concentration of the Church's general infallibility, such as would also govern any meeting of the entire college in a General Council.

So far, so good; and no sensible Catholic should find it very difficult to keep his balance as between these two complementary principles of papacy and 'collegiality'.

But it's easy to lose one's balance, even so, especially at a time of postconciliar trauma; and many of us now talk as though those two principles were not complementary but antithetical. 'Collegiality' can then become a code-word, expressing an antipapal vehemence which the speaker is unwilling to proclaim more candidly.

It often appears to conceal a more specific meaning. "The Pope doesn't seem likely to repeal *Humanae vitae*; but we may be able to twist our local Bishop's arm and make him say that it doesn't really matter or doesn't apply to us." See THE PILGRIM CHURCH.

Ignoble thinking, but bad theology too: there as elsewhere, real 'collegiality' presupposes unity with the See of Peter.

COMMUNISM

At its roots, this word is of course related to 'community' and 'communion'. Its primary reference is to the ideal of shared ownership—of collaboration rather than competition in the use of property. In this sense, 'communism' has been practised in many primitive societies and in the early Church as well (Acts 2:44): it is still practised by many religious orders, sometimes very punctiliously indeed. (I have heard of nuns whose rule forbade them to say "my shoes": it always had to be "our shoes".) Numerous Utopian communities, less monastic and of varying stability, have been organised on more or less communistic lines: sometimes, as in the notorious case of John Humphrey Noyes at Oneida Creek, even wives were held in common.

Apart from such extravagances as that, this pure 'communism' has to be regarded as a noble ideal. If it is to be pursued with any hope of success, two conditions have to be met: there must be a strong religious motivation, and the membership has to be strictly voluntary. Both conditions are met in (say) a good Trappist monastery.

We all know what happens when this previously noble ideal is denied any possible fulfilment of those two conditions and is made atheistic and universal by compulsion. The practical problem is that even when so corrupted into the reverse of an ideal, it can still retain its old power and inspiration, especially in the eyes of the poor. (In them, however, the nobility of the pure ideal is easily damaged by the Deadly Sin of Envy.)

Semantically speaking, 'Communism' then becomes a name and pretext for certain very ancient evils, as practised in our time: tyranny, cruelty, repression, the deification of the system and State and a consequent hostility to every alternative god. We should note, however, that such evils are also practised in societies which are not 'Communist' in any further sense; also, that even within 'Communist' societies, the scale and intensity of their practice can vary enormously.

Thus and otherwise, this is a word of multiple reference. Close attention will show that when some people say 'Communism', they mean little more than 'the Russian Empire and its actual or potential satellites'; and it is of course true that nearly all the evils which we associate with the word were standard practice in the Russia of the Tsars.

The great linguistic danger—as often with such abstract nouns as arouse powerful emotional responses—is that we may reify the concept. 'Communism' then becomes the name of an actual Thing or Being or Entity, monolithic in structure, having its own evil and set purpose, and capable of being seen as an incarnation of Satan within the historical process.

This is a powerful tendency. Men often erect their own verbal constructs into gods (see FREEDOM): they also make them into devils. A Catholic, believing in one God and also in Satan, should be careful to do neither. But that can be a hard job. There's a sub-clinical paranoia latent in all humanity, becoming fully pathological in a few; and such angry passions help it along.

In connection with certain controversies of the day, therefore, it often becomes necessary to say "There's no such thing as Communism", with a certain emphasis on the word "thing". That's not to say that there aren't numerous people who are deluded and wicked in one particular style.

I warn the reader that if he makes that point and opposes the reification of 'Communism', he will be accused of Nominalism—though not by any competent Catholic philosopher.

COMMUNITY

It has become a fashionable cliché that it's the chief business of the Church to 'build community'. This makes perfect sense, but only so long as we use the word carefully. Our task is undoubtedly that of incorporating all men into Christ and so into one another, of building up ('edifying') his Body. Where 'building community' is so understood, nobody can object. But it is often understood in another and very different way.

Generally speaking, a primitive or peasant grows up in a natural but real 'community', economically poor but richly structured: he has his own place within it, he *belongs*, and that's psychologically supportive. By contrast, the big cities of today, although full of consumer-goods, are almost totally unstructured: each is a swirl of unrelated human atoms, with nobody really belonging anywhere or to anyone. This makes *loneliness* into one of the two most agonising social diseases of our time, the other being boredom.

Many most laudable attempts are made to 'build

community' in the sense of easing that loneliness and helping people to belong. Catholics certainly do well when they contribute to such charitable works, but that isn't the specific task of the Church or the priesthood. God did not become incarnate as a remedy for social disintegration, though his following can sometimes—not always—heal those agonies *per accidens*.

It often did so; and it's ironic to see how many present-day Catholics implore us to 'build community' while doing their best to demolish it themselves. In a big city of, say, thirty years ago, the Catholic community was often close and warm and intense, psychologically supportive in the highest degree. But now, what with hyper-ECUMENISM and a passion for OPENNESS—not to mention a widespread loss of faith—we often find it in ruins, torn down by those who claimed to be building.

That can doom the faithful Catholic to a new loneliness.

COUNCIL, THE

When things of broadly the same sort happen again and again but at long intervals, we naturally speak of the most recent instance as though it were the only instance. In my childhood, for example, '*the* war' meant that of 1914 to 1918: in my early manhood, it meant that of 1939 to 1945. We never meant to imply that either was the first or was likely to be the last.

So it's natural, and it should be harmless, to speak of '*the* Council' when we have one particular Council in mind, that of 1962 to 1965. But it isn't altogether harmless in fact: it can involve or suggest endorsement of two very popular delusions, one of them being about Councils in general and the other about that particular Council.

In the first place, we can make the same mistake about Councils as ULTRAMONTANISM makes about the Pope. Papal utterances are weighty things, never to be taken lightly: as Vatican II pointed out, they normally require our inward and outer assent. But they are seldom infallible in the full sense; and as we see from Church history, the practical and prudential judgments of a Pope can sometimes fall short of perfect wisdom. Because a Pope did something, we cannot infer—in any absolute manner—that it was exactly what God wanted done at that particular moment.

So with a General Council. That must always be a momentous happening: a meeting of the entire episcopal college, an assembly of all the Lord's living apostles, or most or many of them at least. In matters of faith and morals, its definitions are like a Pope's: they have to be accepted *de fide*. We there see the finger of God, keeping his Church on the rails.

But . . . let us remember the Fifth Lateran Council. It sat for quite a long time, from 1512 to 1517, and it was as authentically a General Council as any. Its greatest achievement was the creation of certain Catholic pawnshops, the *Monts de Piété*, right across Europe. I find it hard to see that as God's notion of what the Church ought to be doing, more urgently than anything else, just at the moment when Martin Luther was about to burst upon the scene.

The moral ought to be obvious. But beyond that, this most recent Council was the occasion—if not exactly the cause—of a remarkable psychopathological phenomenon, an epidemic of hysteria, a cherished mass-fantasy which is only now beginning to lose its hold over the Catholic mind. Vatican II was a watershed, a New Dispensation in effect! It proposed a total break or discontinuity with the past, it put faith and morals up for grabs, it transferred all Magisterium to the liberal intelligentsia, it caused 'preconciliar' to mean 'outmoded and therefore negligible' when not actually 'corrupt'. That's what many people wanted to believe, anyway, despite what that Council actually did and said; and the excited media gave them every encouragement.

This was not a purely verbal phenomenon, but it had (and has) its consequences for language. Even today, wherever 'the Council!' is said in a certain recognisably euphoric tone of voice, we have to suspect the continuing influence of that pathetically dated hysteria. One remedy is to make a point of saying 'the Second Vatican Council' on every occasion, and in a *relaxed* tone of voice, so indicating that although no triviality, it was—like 'the war'—one among many. Ephesus and Chalcedon and Trent have not been repealed.

It's also a good thing to remind self and others that unless the world is due to end suddenly, we are living through a preconciliar period right now.

When the next Council assembles to weed the garden once again, will it not need to pull up much of what this present generation has been planting in such giddy confidence?

DIGNITY

There are certain controversies which—if we get involved in them—will sooner or later tempt us to speak of human 'dignity'. The abortion controversy is a case in point. But there are others.

Now that's a perfectly respectable word. Its origins, if we go back far enough, lie in the Latin word *decet*, 'it is fitting or appropriate'. The older generation of Catholics will remember the intermediate form *dignus*, which we most emphatically are *not* when it's a question of receiving the Lord. He comes to us in pure love, not because we're fitting and appropriate people to receive him.

As a noun, 'dignity' starts off (in English) as something like 'worth' or 'value'. It then moves on—dangerously—to indicate human attributions of worth or value: titles of nobility, for example, which are not always deserved. A man can be loaded with honours and 'dignities' which are far from being fitting or appropriate for such a scoundrel. The word then goes on to suggest a certain high seriousness of manner, such as we may often observe in someone who has a high opinion of himself. He is dignified: we might even say that he's pompous, possibly to the point of absurdity.

The practical difficulty is that we can hardly use the word 'dignity' today without dragging in irrelevant suggestions of the dignified and even the pompous. Such suggestions are often absurd, especially in connection with the questions that prompt us Catholics to speak up for human 'dignity'.

I am thinking here of the Four Great Moments within the life of man as naturally experienced (the sacraments give us other Great Moments). There's the Great Moment of birth: later on, there can be one shared Great Moment or more of begetting-and-conceiving: from that, there ensues the Great Moment of parturition, which is that of birth as seen from the other side: and finally, we come to the Great Moment of death.

Now on these four occasions, we are far indeed from being dignified or pompous. All but the second are in fact medical occasions: we are reduced to patients, suffering animals, forfeiting all command over our own destiny, and with blood commonly involved. We writhe and sweat, we aren't the least bit dignified. As for the second, let Sir Thomas Browne speak: "It is the foolishest act a wise man commits in all his life; nor is there anything that will more deject his cool'd imagination, when he shall consider what an odd and unworthy piece of folly he hath committed." We may rightly reject the Manichaean or Swiftian contempt for the body which is there implied. But it remains true that when two people concelebrate the liturgy of Venus, their lack of 'dignity' is just about total. They are behaving exactly like two pigs in a shed, even though sacramentally.

I suggest that we should refrain altogether from speaking of human 'dignity' in any such connection. The best alternative word would seem to be 'value'—in God's sight, that is, since some human lives are of no human value.

But we shall still need to be careful. Value? It costs God nothing to make a new human being or a new galaxy. If it comes to that, it costs us nothing to make a new human being: the first stage of that operation is widely reported to be positively enjoyable.

It's only the price-tag of Christ's blood which gives to each human life a value or 'dignity' which —if not infinite—is certainly incapable of being quantified.

ECUMENISM

Some years ago, it was fashionable to speak of 'O.K.-words'. A word was deemed to be 'O.K.' if it could be trusted to elicit a knee-jerk response of the most positive sort—perhaps universally, or perhaps within specified circles alone. It carried a warm emotional loading; which was nice for the word but unpropitious for any hope of clear thinking.

As a noun and in adjectival form, 'ecumenism' has recently become very much of an O.K.-word, and not only in religious circles: the unbeliever, impatiently sarcastic about 'the Churches', will commonly say that they should at least be 'ecumenical'. The antonyms of that adjective—'un-ecumenical', 'divisive', 'dogmatic', and so forth—are regarded as dirty words in almost every quarter. Their application damns.

We have here another case of ambiguity, concealed from many by the O.K.-status of the word.

Let it be granted (but see CHURCH) that CHRISTIANITY comes before the world in a number of versions, institutionally distinct and differing among themselves in various further ways: let them here be called the 'denominations'. Their existence raises two quite separate questions.

a. What should be the relationship between them? In the past, it has often been a tense, angry, and contemptuous relationship, involving many persecutions and religious wars. In one sense, 'ecumenism' is an attempt to replace that hostility with friendship, mutual understanding, and various kinds of collaboration; and with various local exceptions—in and around Belfast, for example—it's it's an attempt that has now reached almost total success.

b. But should these separate 'denominations' exist *at all*? Didn't the Lord want his followers to be "one"? And don't their present separations strengthen the unbeliever's case? "If after nearly two thousand years, you Christians *still* can't agree about what it is that you're saying and offering to the world, how can any of you be taken seriously?" In a second sense, 'ecumenism' is an attempt to disarm that powerful objection by eliminating these visible divisions and enabling all Christians to speak with one voice; and in this sense, it's an attempt that shows practically no sign of ever succeeding.

See UNITY, CHRISTIAN. The trouble is that we cannot attach any coherent meaning to that expression that won't be controversial, and in that sense divisive, and in that sense unecumenical.

So the word 'ecumenism' needs to become less O.K. That's a concept with serious built-in limitations, unless we confine it to that first sense of better relations all round. In the second sense, it's self-defeating.

ENCOUNTER

Somebody once asked a group of Catholic schoolgirls whether confession—the Rite of Reconciliation, if you prefer—was experienced by themselves as a real 'encounter' with Christ. As with one voice, they replied that it was not. Bad news?

A few years ago, this was a vogue-word of the utmost popularity among such Catholics as desired to seem progressive above all else. It often went along with MEANINGFUL. But like that silly word, it now seems to have fallen out of fashion.

Good riddance if so. That was always a word that made for confusion. The trouble appears to have been that it was taken over, in rather unexamined quasi-literal haste, from the French word *rencontre(r)*, which was then in vogue as a way of urging a more personal, less abstract relationship with the Lord. But although moderately distant relatives, the two words are in sharp semantic contrast. The French word has the primary sense of 'a meeting' or 'to meet': it can carry some suggestion of hostility or collision, but only in a secondary and occasional manner. But that kind of suggestion predominates in the English word, it comes first. You 'meet' a good friend, but you 'encounter' opposition or an obstacle: two armies 'encounter' one another on the field of battle.

Those girls will have understood the question in terms of whether they experienced confession as some kind of fight with the Lord and against him; and in their piety, they knew that it was more like a surrender to him, a laying-down of their rebellious arms. They answered correctly, giving no cause for alarm.

High fashion is commonly associated with a kind of excitement that can easily falsify understanding and judgment. Beware of vogue-words.

EXPERIENCE

Some people like to speak of 'religious experiences'. I suspect that the greatest of these—the most deeply religious, the most crucially evidential—is the mere experience of existing, of being alive. The trouble is that people don't always recognise it *as* a religious experience.

Beyond that, one needs to be careful. Here's an extreme case. I once took part in an all-night radio show at New York, the subject being contraception. I gave various reasons for regarding it as morally evil.

But I was facing a man who had left the Catholic priesthood and got 'married', and he disagreed vehemently. "Look, I've *experienced* its moral goodness!"

He presumably meant that it gave him no qualms of conscious GUILT. But if true, that was just a psychological fact about himself. 'Experience', in that sense, is no reliable guide to anything.

Many of us, not only the great mystics, have 'experienced' moments of high spiritual exaltation, during which it seemed that we were piercing to the heart of all things and almost beholding the face of God. Such moments are frequent in certain lives, and they are sometimes more shattering than enjoyable. Some people, being so favoured by God, have been mightily strengthened in faith thereby, even transformed.

It would be shameful to play down the reality and importance of such 'experiences', or of the more humdrum 'experiences' that we undergo in the course of our pilgrimage.

A certain care is needed, even so. It's rather as with private revelations. As we all know, certain people have been favoured with apparitions of our Lady, or of our Lord and the Saints. That's true. But it's also true that other people, being insane or possessed or both, have had delusions of being so favoured. By their fruits you shall know them. Where such an 'experience' is followed by utterances that clash with the mind of the Church, it must be regarded with the deepest distrust.

So with all other more or less spiritual 'experiences'. The trouble is that, for the person concerned, they can seem totally self-validating. "Don't argue with me! I've been there, I *know*!"— a claim which may or may not be justified. So it's important to remember the tortuosity of the human mind, the allure of self-deception and even the power of Satan.

The semantic difficulty is that many non-Catholics assume that 'experience' is more or less synonymous with 'faith' or 'religion'—that where we aspire to make converts, we are seeking above all else to share our personal 'experiences' with others. They find it hard to take in the fact that we're mostly talking about something far more objective. So this also is a word that needs watching.

FAITH

In legend or in fact, there was once a schoolboy who—when asked for a definition—said, "Faith is believing something which you know to be untrue." For many unbelievers, that comes close to the mark: 'faith', for them, is an irrationality so total as to approach dishonesty.

In the long history of the word, since the Reformation especially, there are elements which explain that cynicism and may even justify it in certain contexts.

As theologically used, this word has two distinct and incompatible meanings. The difference between them is best defined in terms of the relationship between 'faith', on the one hand, and 'intellect' or 'reason' on the other—though each of those two latter words has its own semantic and historical complexity and can easily be misunderstood when encountered nowadays in some ancient text.

Here's the difference, as broadly stated. On the old Protestant view, 'faith' and 'reason' are mutually irrelevant at the best, mutually hostile at the worst. But on the Catholic view, they are mutually supportive.

Other statements of the case are possible. Is the 'act of faith' a leap in the dark? Or is it a leap from *some* light into a much greater light? Alternatively: Is it an act of the pure will, unrelated to any sort of reasoning? or is it an act of the will *as directed by the intellect*?

I don't suppose that in that historic version, the question comes in for much present-day discussion. Perhaps it should: when brushed aside, it becomes one of the numerous factors that frustrate the brave hopes of ECUMENISM.

Its controversial past certainly makes 'faith' into a dangerously ambiguous word. In post-Protestant societies, especially when English-speaking, most people assume without question that it refers to something wholly irrational, wholly subjective, and chiefly a matter of 'EXPERIENCES' and 'feelings'. As a Catholic controversialist, I have constantly found it practically impossible to put across the idea that, rightly or wrongly, we don't see 'faith' in those terms. We claim to be speaking about something wholly objective, the actual grain and structure of reality, very much as explored by the scientist—though his verification-method is naturally unlike ours.

'Faith'? When we call that a virtue, most people

assume us to mean "Trust your innermost and sacred feelings, even in the teeth of reasoned argument and the most obviously factual evidence" —which comes close to that schoolboy's cynical definition. In fact, we mean something more like "Trust the hard evidence provided by Christ in his Church, even in the teeth of your own innermost feelings." The hardness of that evidence is always in principle—and often in fact—a matter of previous intellectual judgment, even though followed by a choice and commitment, an act of the will.

A word makes trouble when it acquires two contradictory meanings. One practical difficulty is that if a Catholic lives in a post-Protestant society, he can easily and quite unconsciously absorb its vocabulary, its semantics. His use and understanding of this word 'faith' can then be skewed: common usage will tend to pull it away from the Catholic sense which he intends, and confusion will then follow. It would sort itself out if he paid close attention to words and meanings. But some of us are ill-qualified to do that, and some of us can't be bothered to try.

"Whom do you have good reason to trust?" That's one soundly Catholic statement of the case. Experience, if not academic psychology, should tell us that innermost feelings are very untrustworthy indeed.

FREEDOM (or LIBERTY)

The Old Testament prophets used to thunder against idolatry, and with good cause. You and I feel no temptation to worship idols of wood or stone, and we may therefore feel immune to this temptation. If so, that's rash of us. We commit idolatry whenever we make anything short of God into an absolute. The man-made gods (and devils) of this generation are mostly conceptual and verbal, very seldom physical; and in respect of them, that old temptation is still with us.

'Freedom' or 'liberty' is a case in point: a good value within limits, but no kind of absolute or god. Both words, and others like them, originally signified the legal condition of not being a slave, someone's property. Today they have three chief references—political, academic and religious.

Take 'political freedom', which is constantly mentioned as though it were the name of a god. It was not deified by the Gospels or the Church, however, but by the eighteenth-century 'Enlightenment' and the romantic and revolutionary enthusiasms that followed. Our traditionally Catholic sources give absolutely no indication that politics is a supremely important subject, or that 'freedom' or 'liberty' is supreme among the various kinds of political good. Poor people have usually cared more about security: our Catholic writers have usually laid more emphasis upon order, hierarchy and obedience. To make 'freedom' into anything like an absolute is to exalt each individual's assertive ego, whereas Christ was made obedient for us right up to the death of the Cross. He didn't do his own thing.

'Academic freedom'. Much present-day controversy stems from the fact that where this is made into an absolute, the idea of 'a Catholic university' seems to be a contradiction in terms. We should remember that 'academic freedom' is never claimed or conceded except where uncertainty still prevails. The professor of mathematics cannot claim it to justify his teaching that $2 + 2 = 17$; and it suffers no violation if you fail to get a teaching post in astronomy or geography because of your belief in the old Ptolemaic cosmogony or a flat earth. Well, where *does* uncertainty still prevail? Any university has to presuppose some sort of answer to that question. If *all* things are still uncertain, neither research nor teaching will be honestly possible. A Catholic university, like any other, has its own definition of where certainty does and does not exist: there's no contradiction.

What about 'religious freedom'? As against the State, I feel most passionately that this needs to be absolute—but with a certain nervousness, since wiser and holier men than myself have felt otherwise. At the time of the Reformation, it was agreed on practically all sides that the Christian Prince had the duty to stamp out heresy and promote true religion: only the distinguishing and identification of the two were in dispute.

However that may be, 'religious freedom' before God and one's own conscience is a most dangerous concept. "Everyone has a right to believe what he likes!" Has he? a right to conform his intellect to his wishes? It's a prime moral duty to conform one's mind to *reality*, and to suspend judgment where reality seems inaccessible. The freedom to do otherwise is a freedom in dishonesty and self-deception.

So let's respect 'freedom' without making it into a god. The false gods have a habit of requiring human sacrifice, and political 'freedom'—where deified—seems more than likely to require a holocaust of millions.

Within our Catholic vocabulary, these words 'freedom' and 'liberty' need to be kept in their place. We should not give them the quasi-divine status that they enjoy elsewhere. There's only one God.

GAY

In general, semantic change has to be accepted, understood and allowed for. Efforts to resist it are usually wasted.

But there are cases in which the free use of a word in some new sense will 'give scandal' by suggesting connivance in evil. This is a case in point. Its current popularity, in the sense of 'homosexual', appears to stem from two factors. People are reluctant to seem 'judgmental' by any application of adversative language to others: they also feel that in this matter, adversative language would be inappropriate as well as rudely and proudly judgmental. What's so wrong about being 'gay'? It's only 'love'—that supreme value—in a slightly different version!

Moralistic comment would be superfluous. But so far as vocabulary is concerned, we should remember that objective or value-free words are available. We are told not to judge others, and there is a case for avoiding sharply adversative terms. But we needn't go to the other extreme and use terms that carry highly positive loadings, as 'gay' has done from the start. You *endorse* something when you associate it, verbally and in the most arbitrary manner, with lighthearted cheerfulness.

Let us remember, however, that this present use of that word is not a total novelty. In seventeenth-century English, it could mean 'dissipated' or—as they used to say—'fast', with a clear note of moral rebuke; and two centuries later, in the supposedly prim Victorian age, a 'gay' woman could be, quite simply, a prostitute.

In this connection, it is a pity that so many Catholics confuse the two senses of 'homosexuality'. It can refer to a mere proclivity for which the individual may not be to blame, a temptation in fact: it can also refer to the indulgence of that proclivity, the habit of yielding to that temptation. The difference is important. I have known priests of the most self-controlled and saintly sort in whom the proclivity was manifest and the temptation doubtlessly powerful. They deserved no rebuke.

GUILT

We Catholics are sometimes accused of being morbidly obsessed with guilt, pathologically anxious about our own sinfulness. Worse still (they say), we positively encourage our children in guilt-neurosis: that's asking for trouble.

Here and there, such accusations may well be justified—less often today, perhaps, than in certain past ages. But the consideration of these questions is frequently bedevilled by semantic confusion. That word 'guilt' has five distinct meanings, and they need to be distinguished at every point.

In the first sense, that word refers to pure fact, often to pure physical fact. Did you actually do it? Was it really your finger that pulled the trigger? The moralists speak here of 'material guilt'.

In the second place, 'guilt' can refer to moral blame or culpability. Was it with full knowledge that you did this wicked thing, and with the full consent of your will? The lawyers speak here of *mens rea* and the moralists of 'formal guilt', which is what can damn you.

Note that these first two guilts are independent of one another. If I attempt to seduce some young lady but fail—what with her virtue, or her common sense, or her good taste—I incur the full 'formal guilt' of an adultery that never happened 'materially'. Conversely, any number of factors can mitigate, or even eliminate, the 'formal guilt' of something that I actually did. The law recognises this: a verdict of 'guilty but insane' means "He did it, but he cannot be held responsible."

Thirdly, 'guilt' can occasionally mean 'repentance'. This has two components: an intellectual recognition that you have done something wrong and a resolution—an act of the will—to do better in the future, with the help of God's grace. There is no necessary involvement of the feelings or emotions.

Fourthly, 'guilt' can very often mean 'remorse'. This definitely does involve the emotions: it's a kind of horrified disgust at what you did, possibly coupled with an *ad hoc* element of self-hatred. In a healthy mind, genuine repentance will usually be accompanied by an element of remorse. But that isn't of primary importance. For psychological reasons, people vary enormously in their emotional responses to their own perceived wickedness; and where a penitent is shocked by their feebleness within himself, it's usually a mistake for him to use willpower and imagination in the hope of working them up to some greater intensity. He should repent, using his intellect and his will: he should allow his emotions to whirl around in their own uncontrollable and unimportant manner.

Fifthly and finally, 'guilt' can often mean 'repentance' or 'remorse' (or both) when obsessively disproportionate. In the first case, it's what the moralists call 'scrupulosity': "Father, I'm damned —I put three spoonfuls of sugar in my breakfast coffee this morning instead of two." But it's in the second case that the word shows its greatest power of generating confusion, with popular psychology carrying most of the blame. Yes, you did something wicked. But that was long ago; and you're still tormented by the memory of it. It obsesses you, it darkens your whole life, you can't think about anything else: you lose all faith in God's power to forgive and even in people's power to forget. You're then in a pathological state, and the therapist may or may not be able to help you.

The practical difficulty is that any discussion of 'guilt' tends to bog down in the word's ambiguity and to be overshadowed by that highly specialised sense of obsession and neurosis. Moral: distinguish carefully at every point.

Yes, popular psychology has a lot to answer for. 'Guilt' isn't always a pathological delusion, as some people appear to suppose: it's often an ugly fact. That's where we Catholics have the advantage, since we know how to put it right.

HERESY

Within our present-day Catholic vocabulary, this word still exists but is of curiously ambiguous respectability. We may invoke it freely in connection with the safely distant past: no cheek will blush if we mention the Arian 'heresy'. But any current application of that word, to people now living, will be widely regarded as a shocking impropriety. Why should this be?

It isn't as though Arianism had ceased to exist. At any gathering of vaguely Christian people, even of ill-instructed Catholics, you will often find the Lord seen in precisely Arian terms: if you listen carefully, you will in fact catch echoes of all the ancient christological heresies and many another. But they no longer exist corporately or institutionally: there isn't an Arian Church whose members will take offence at any slur.

That may be part of the explanation. We should also remember that thanks to various ugly episodes in the past, the word 'heretic' still carries inescapable overtones of 'somebody who ought to be burned at the stake.' That may well make people hypersensitive about it.

Even so, that ambiguity is an odd thing. We would make one kind of sense if we said that there never was such a thing as 'heresy', in the fourth century or earlier or later, and that the word should therefore be dropped altogether: that would be straight agnosticism. But it makes little sense to say that while it once existed and was a serious matter, it has now lost its reality or its importance or both.

But nobody actually says that. The fact is that the subject has simply become unmentionable, just as sexual matters once were in certain circles.

This is presumably because of ECUMENISM: 'heresy' is clearly a divisive concept, and in that sense unecumenical.

But a curious paradox arises here. Ecumenism calls upon all Christians (but see CHRISTIANITY) to make the most of their common inheritance and the least of what divides them. But a major part of their common inheritance is a deep conviction that it is very easy to get Christianity wrong and very important to get it right. They disagreed for centuries, often violently, about what constituted 'heresy': about its very great evil, they were all in accord until very recently. In that sense as in some others, ecumenism requires us to be unecumenical.

When great evils become unmentionable, they also become irremediable. If a shy young girl cannot bear to mention her intimate symptoms to a male doctor, he won't be able to help her.

As we all know, the word 'heresy' comes from a Greek word which means 'selectivity' or 'picking and choosing'. Where two men meet as equals, it can be good manners and good morality to say "I agree with much of what you say, but I'm not buying all of it." That isn't so good, however, when said by a grossly ignorant man to some great scholar in the relevant field; and it's morally and intellectually outrageous when said by men to God.

But has God said anything coherent? Where 'heresy' is allowed to become a dirty word, the clear implication is that he has not.

If Christianity isn't something which people can get wrong, it can't be something which people can get right. It then becomes a zero-thing.

It's probably too late to rehabilitate the word 'heresy', however carefully and courteously we might contrive to use it. Will somebody please find an alternative word, still adversative—it should curdle one's blood to think of anyone picking and choosing among the sternly luminous oracles of God!—but not tainted with the memory of ancient cruelties?

I can't think of such a word. Maybe the old one will have to serve—unless, of course, we follow the overriding principle of never saying anything adversative or corrective about anybody.

That wasn't the style of Jesus.

INSIGHT

In mediaeval English, this word referred to any vision or perception that was mental rather than visual. Its present-day usage is very similar. You get an 'insight' into something when you come to understand it.

But the word usually carries two further implications. One is of *novelty*. We seldom speak of an 'insight' when a schoolboy comes to understand something old and already familiar to others. But we might well use that word when a scientist notices and understands something entirely new about (say) DNA or the electron.

The word also carries an implication of *presumptive rightness*. On the basis of his 'insight', that scientist might well formulate a new hypothesis, such as might survive experimental testing. But if it broke down under test and proved to be a mistaken hypothesis—like many others in the history of science—we would no longer use the word 'insight' when we mentioned its formulation in the past tense. We would be more likely to speak of that scientist's 'mistake'.

An 'insight' is correct by definition. In that, it differs sharply from 'hypothesis' or 'opinion'.

Now in certain Catholic circles, it has become fashionable to use this word in connection with the hypotheses or opinions of favoured theologians. It then implies a confidence which is not always warranted, and indeed a certain arrogance. "Dr. X thinks so-and-so": that's fair enough, as is "and I tend to agree with him." But one needs to be very sure of oneself before adding "and he's quite certainly right", which is implied by any use of 'insight' in that connection. Novelty, yes: presumptive rightness, no. A theologian deals only in hypotheses; and like those of the scientist, these often turn out to be dead ends or delusions, 'mistakes' rather than 'insights'.

To some degree, this problem arises because of a widespread desire that theology should be an autonomous and cumulatively developing science, in which the new—if not presumptively right in any absolute sense—will usually be closer to the mark than what went before. Things are like that in the natural sciences, and—sometimes, much more precariously—in the humanities. But in theology, when considered as an academic discipline, things can't be like that at all.

The popularity of this word 'insight', as now used by too many Catholics, is an ugly phenomenon. It reflects a willingness to use question-begging rhetoric in order to reinforce cherished certainties that aren't really there.

An *arrogant* word: avoid it.

LOVE

The crucial importance of this concept and word, for faith and morals and indeed for all human life, needs no emphasis by myself.

What does need emphasis is the complexity of the concept and therefore of the word as well. 'Love' comes (or fails to come) in many versions: the word has various different and sometimes conflicting senses. A married man 'loves' his pretty secretary: will he therefore seduce her? or will he leave her strictly alone? It depends on what is there meant by 'love'.

The practical difficulty is that in most present-day discourse, the erotic and affective senses of the word are overwhelmingly dominant, so that its crucifying sense of *agape*—where intended—can easily be overlooked. The consequent cross-purposes, unless remedied, will tend to dissolve faith into sentimentality and virtue into perversion.

This is *not* a word to be thrown around carelessly, as so often by so many of us.

MARRIAGE

This word is currently used in two quite distinct senses. Each is defensible in its own context, but it's important not to confuse them.

In most present-day contexts, it refers to an institution which is common to practically all human societies, though the anthropologist knows of a few tiny exceptions. It may be defined as 'regular cohabitation', more or less permanent by intention at least, when given some degree of social and customary or legal recognition. It is usually monogamous, sometimes polygamous, occasionally polyandrous. One might argue that the expression 'GAY marriage', though morally outrageous, is linguistically acceptable: it conveys a clear meaning.

But in the Catholic vocabulary, 'marriage' has a further sense. It naturally refers to a heterosexual and monogamous relationship alone, but also to one which has a sacramental or organic quality which only death can extinguish.

That word 'can' is important. Some people talk as though the Church *forbade* divorce in a rather heartless manner and should make exceptions in those hard cases which undoubtedly exist. But that isn't quite accurate. What the Church says is that God forbids adultery, and that divorce—in any full sense—is not wrong but factually impossible. So long as we both live, I can no more stop being my wife's husband than I can stop being my sister's brother. Each relationship is objective, unaffected by any words or rituals of the legal sort.

For greater accuracy, let us remember that this only applies to a VALID and consummated marriage between baptised people; and the word 'consummated' should remind us that in this full Catholic sense, we don't get inescapably 'married' in church but in bed. What happens in church is a public declaration, before God and man, of the sacramental terms on which we shall soon be going to bed.

The difference between these two senses of 'marriage' is not so very obscure or pedantic: it's the difference between a social or conventional arrangement and a factually sacramental and organic relationship. One might compare it to the difference between a business partnership (which can be broken) and that biological relationship between brother and sister (which cannot, though its legal consequences can).

I am not the first to suggest that it would be helpful if this difference were recognised in common speech, so that we all knew which of our friends were 'married' in the full Catholic sense and which in the socially conventional sense alone. It might be made explicit in the ceremony itself: ". . . and I expressly repudiate any rights of divorce that are conferred by existing legislation or may be conferred by future legislation, within this country or elsewhere." That is of course the real sense of our existing ceremony. But it might help to avoid confusion if it were made even more explicit and legally watertight, so that any subsequent 'marriage'—even after legal divorce—would lay one open to a charge of bigamy. Semantically speaking, that would help to resolve the word's present ambiguity.

See NULLITY.

MASS

Strictly speaking, this word refers to the eucharistic liturgy of the Latin or Western Church alone. In the Eastern Churches, whether Orthodox or Uniate, 'Liturgy' is the appropriate word (but see CHURCH). To speak of 'the Mass of St. John Chrysostom' is a solecism, though a very forgiveable one.

I have never been entirely convinced by the conventional explanations of that word 'Mass' and (behind it) of *Missa*. It seems unlikely, though not altogether impossible, that the whole rite should have been named after its concluding words of dismissal. When you invite people to a party or dinner, you don't call it a 'goodbye', and it's hard to imagine the semantic process that could ever cause you to do so. Could *Missa* have been influenced by the phonetic proximity of *mensa*, a table?

However that may be, two things are clear

about this somewhat obscure word: it comes from Latin, and it has long implied a strong emphasis upon the sacrificial nature of the eucharistic rite. At the time of the Reformation and subsequently, a 'massing-priest' was sharply and often adversatively distinguished from a Protestant *presbyter*, who—although he did preside at the Lord's Supper—saw his primary task as that of preaching the word.

Both factors appear to be involved in the *shyness* with which the word 'Mass' now fills certain Catholics, their eagerness to speak of 'a Liturgy' or 'a Eucharist' instead. By association of ideas—hardly by any sort of logic—the Latin word suggests Rome and therefore the Pope, where either of those two Greek words would not: it also carries that strongly sacrificial loading. It's a divisive word, therefore, and something of an embarrassment to those who erect ECUMENISM into an absolute value.

The Mass defines itself as an act of thanksgiving (*Gratias agamus* . . .), and we need not be reluctant to call it a *Eucharistia*: its celebrant (see CELEBRATION) is a *leitourgos* or public servant among other things, and we may properly call it by a name which comes close to meaning 'public works'. But any careful avoidance of 'Mass' is a bad sign. It suggests a passion which I am often tempted to understand in terms of neurosis—that is to say, a blind passion for discontinuity with the Catholic past (see COUNCIL). It also suggests a related and equally blind passion for any sort of ecumenism on any sort of terms.

A prudent Catholic will feel free to use any one of those three words, according to the emphasis required in each specific context. But he will not allow it to be supposed that the Latin and more specifically Catholic word causes him even the faintest embarrassment.

It may be of some interest (though of no importance) to note that in England, the pronunciation of 'Mass' can be an indicator of class or region or both. Where the *a* is lengthened, the suggestion is of old recusant nobility or of northern origin. Being no aristocrat and a southerner, I instinctively keep it short. But I'm prepared to be very ecumenical about that.

MEANINGFUL

A book called *The Meaning of Meaning* once attracted considerable attention. It perplexed one critic so much that he headed his review 'The Meaning of *The Meaning of Meaning*'.

Ignoring those philosophical depths, we can observe two distinct senses in which 'mean' is used in common speech. "What does it mean to be an American citizen?" We answer that question in terms of a legal status, conferred by birth or naturalisation. But if I varied the formula and asked "What does your American citizenship mean to you?", I would be asking a different kind of question: it would need to be answered in terms of your emotional responses to that status.

That distinction carries over into the use, and the very frequent abuse, of the vogue-word 'meaningful'.

As far as I can see, it was first put into circulation by the Logical Positivists. In order to be

MEANINGFUL

meaningful, they said, a proposition had to be either analytic or else empirically verifiable: if it was neither, it was meaningless in the most obvious sense, amounting to nothing more than gibberish. That meant that metaphysicians and theologians talked nothing but drivel: it also meant, to the delight of many, that Logical Positivists talked nothing but drivel. They became very angry with those who pointed this out.

Despite the intellectual suicide of those philosophasters, there is a case for the word 'meaningful'. Between the propositions 'The cat sat on the mat' and 'Qwert yuiop', there is a real difference which can do with an adjectival label, though I'd prefer it to be less cumbersome.

But the word is seldom used in that strict sense. As a jargon-word (which is what it has mostly become), it indicates little more than an emotional response, positive in nature but otherwise unspecified.

There are some, for example—in the wrath of God—who like to speak of 'a truly meaningful liturgy' (see MASS). What do they mean? Hardly that its various symbolisms were perfectly understood by themselves at every point: only that they liked it. It made them feel good. (The Mass is traditionally said to serve four ends or purposes, to do four things: I don't remember that 'making people feel good' was among them. But that's another question.)

One could ring the changes on this theme. Catholics have traditionally asked whether sexual acts were virtuous or sinful: there are some who ask whether they're meaningful or not, and one can only guess at what they suppose themselves to be meaning. Enjoyable? Efficacious as psychotherapy? Capable of building up a meaningful relationship, whatever that may be?

But one shouldn't really kick a man when he's down; and I hope and trust that after a long period of ascendancy, 'meaningful' is at last on the way down. It's so obviously a non-word, it isn't meaningful.

Jargon is what people use for plugging the holes in their thought.

NULLITY

There's a widespread and usually unshakeable belief that this word—as found in the Catholic vocabulary—is only a fancy euphemism for 'divorce', as conceded to rich and powerful people by a Church which doesn't want to admit that she's there breaking her own rules.

This is nonsense, of course. It's one thing to say that Hitler is dead: it's quite another thing to say that Hitler never existed at all. (The end-result is the same: Hitler isn't alive now. But those two assertions remain sharply different.)

So with a Christian marriage. It's one thing—and an *empty* thing—to speak of terminating it: it's quite another thing to ask whether it ever really existed at all. Appearances can be deceptive.

In this connection, the relationship between brother and sister can provide a useful analogy once again (see MARRIAGE). From time to time, a legal problem (usually concerning inheritance) requires the courts to decide whether two people really *are* brother and sister or not. That question calls for an enquiry of the essentially historical sort, into the possible reality of a biological event that may or may not have happened many years ago: it has to be conducted on the ordinary principles of historical research and legal evidence, and while the court *may* attain unquestionable certainty, it will often have to decide on a balance of probabilities.

That's a fairly close analogy to what the Church does in a nullity case; and it has nothing whatever to do with the question of whether these two people would be happier with different partners or not.

It's a sad fact that in proceedings of the judicial or quasi-judicial sort, rich people will commonly have an advantage over poor people. But in this matter of nullity, that's less true now than it sometimes has been.

But it's as well to remember that the moral perfection of ecclesiastical officials and tribunals forms no part of Catholic faith.

OPENNESS

Certain Catholics, when telling us how much more splendid everything is than it was before the Second Vatican COUNCIL, like to speak of "a new openness to the world".

I often wonder what they suppose themselves to mean. The Church was always wide open to the world, she invited, she implored. "Come right in, everybody, and make yourselves at home!": the door was never shut.

But they may be thinking of open-mindedness; and there, they have a certain limited point. It's more than merely arguable that since the Counter-Reformation—and especially since the original Modernist movement of a hundred years ago—the Church's necessary doctrinal discipline was exercised in an unnecessarily rigid and crabbed manner, as though approved formulae told all and as though intellectual exploration would most certainly lead to heresy. It can do so, but it needn't.

Today, by way of overreaction, that discipline hardly appears to be exercised at all. A happy medium is possible and—surely?—desirable.

Catholics thus acquired the reputation of having closed minds. But in what sense is that a bad thing? As Chesterton said so memorably, "The only purpose of opening the mind, as of opening the mouth, is to shut it again on something solid." But is there anything solid for the mind to eat? Not if the agnostics are right.

I fear that when the postconciliar Church is praised for her "new openness to the world", the thing admired is a willingness of certain Catholics to talk as though they were agnostics—as though all things were now uncertain and in flux, but also as though the intellectual fashion of the passing moment commanded tremendous respect. Even if I lost the Faith, I couldn't possibly respect *that*.

Can we define the senses in which the mind of a Catholic, and of the Church as a whole, should— and should not—be 'open to the world'? I think we can, neatly but at the cost of a certain vulgarity. It's excellent and necessary for the Catholic mind to be 'open' to new thinking, but only if it's open *at both ends*, like the alimentary canal. It can then welcome all manner of miscellaneous ideas, taking them in, subjecting them to a process of digestion that may well be slow, and assimilating whatever it finds congenial to its own nature and life; and it can then . . . well, *eliminate* the useless remainder.

That's the norm. Take no offence! The Lord himself spoke of excretion (Mt 15:17).

For the life of Christ's Body the Church, organic metaphors are usually the best; and that's a good organic metaphor for what the Church did (for example) to Aristotle, with Saint Thomas there enacting the role of the digestive juices. Some people want to see Karl Marx given the same treatment: my suspicion is that practically no part of him would prove digestible. The two cases are not parallel, since the pagan Aristotle was a deeply religious man.

That metaphor, in all its earthiness, provides us with an accurate if indelicate label for bad theologians.

They abound most noisily. When I consider the effective absence of any doctrinal discipline from today's Catholic scene, I am sometimes tempted to write a book called *The Constipated Church*.

But of course, that would never do. That subject, freely mentioned by God Incarnate, is still likely to offend pious ears.

PEOPLE OF GOD, THE

This expression has scriptural origins of the most respectable sort, though the Lord preferred to speak of his 'Kingdom'. The Church may certainly be described as 'a People', successor in title to 'the Chosen People' of the old Dispensation, but 'catholic' in the primary sense of being for all men, subject to no ethnic or national or political circumscription.

None the less, this is an expression that needs careful watching. In recent times, the word 'people' has acquired new overtones, democratic and egalitarian and even Marxist in tendency, such as were totally absent from its scriptural usage. Those who speak frequently of 'the People of God' will therefore be making quasi-political suggestions in that sense, whether by conscious intention or inadvertently: in particular, they will be making antihierarchical suggestions. They may not fully and frankly desire to see the apostolic Magisterium and governance handed over to a majority vote of all such people as choose to call themselves 'Catholics' (see CATHOLIC): they will certainly give aid and comfort to those who do so desire.

Within strict limits, there's a case for that desire: it can suggest a usefully corrective manner of thinking. Some of us overreact rather absurdly from all such suggestions of an egalitarian and democratic Church and soar to heights of ULTRAMONTANISM that were effectively condemned in 1870. It is no rare thing to meet a Catholic who treats some question as entirely open simply because no current or recent Pope has seen fit to make an *ex cathedra* pronouncement about it. We should all remember that certain Popes have come close to heresy, and more generally, that shepherds can sometimes go astray while sheep do not. The history of Arianism illustrates that possibility, and so can a present-day diocese or parish.

But there's danger in any turn of phrase which attributes an implied normality to any such exceptional situation. I suggest, therefore, that while we may lawfully speak of 'the People of God', we should not do so invariably or with any great emphasis. More or less alternately, perhaps, we should use other expressions as well. The word 'Kingdom' has its own political overtones, of course, but as against those of 'people', these are of a converse and therefore counterbalancing sort.

There's no harm in speaking habitually of 'the Church' (but see CHURCH).

We should certainly not be embarrassed by the word 'hierarchical', which is in some ways antithetical to 'egalitarian' or 'popular'—though it's no mere pun to observe that hierarchy can be a very popular thing. That word's most common reference is to the ecclesiastical hierarchy of Pope and bishops and priests and deacons and laity, but it has further reference to the very foundations of our Faith. Even Heaven itself, the perfect society, is traditionally seen in hierarchical terms, though never (of course) with any suggestion of aristocratic arrogance at the highest level or of resentful proletarian envy at the lowest. Love takes keen delight in obedience and subordination—a fact which many people, if they grasp it at all, can only understand in pathological terms.

Either way, of course—egalitarianism *vs.* hierarchy—we must remember that no strictly political doctrine is entailed by our Faith.

One sort of priest likes to advertise a 'People's Mass'. To the literal mind, that carries a ludicrous suggestion that the other Masses are for frogs or giraffes. But as more seriously intended, it carries an unpleasant suggestion of class-conflict. Like every other kind of conflict, that has no place at Mass.

PERSON

This is a curious word, since it goes into the plural in two distinct ways.

A lift or elevator will sometimes carry a sign that reads "To carry not more than eight persons" —human beings, that is, and presumably adults. But that particular plural is seldom used except in two specialised contexts—in trinitarian theology and in certain legal documents. (For the lawyer, a 'person' isn't necessarily a human being.) Elsewhere, we usually say 'people', which comes from a different root and isn't inherently plural at all: we can speak of 'a people' (see PEOPLE OF GOD) and also of different 'peoples'.

No trouble arises there. But in present-day usage as affecting us Catholics, 'person' calls for suspicious vigilance.

Its original sense of 'an actor's mask' and so of 'an act or pretence' has long been forgotten. In the English language, it has carried the clear and simple sense of 'a human being' since the thirteenth century at least, with just those two more specialised senses in theology and law. Along with the related word 'personality', it is of course capable of philosophical analysis. But for all daily purposes, its plain sense needs to be borne in mind.

The trouble is that it's starting to acquire a new sense. Some of us now use it to mean, not 'a human being' *simpliciter*, but something like 'a human being who has reached a certain stage of development and maturity'. In this new sense, we can speak of somebody 'becoming a person' or 'becoming more fully a person' when he already is a 'person' in the older sense, and completely. (A parallel development allows us to speak of a human being becoming 'more fully human'.)

Now semantic change is a fact of linguistic life and can seldom be held back. But it needs to be watched, recognised, allowed for. If I utter some word in an old sense and you understand it in some newer sense, we shall be at cross-purposes. Worse still, I may be able to coerce you into saying something that you don't mean: ambiguity always carries that danger, and wicked people take advantage of it.

It's in connection with abortion, of course, that the current ambiguity of 'person' is most dangerous. Consider an unborn child, perhaps two months after conception. Is he or she a 'person'? In the old sense, yes: we are speaking of a human being, a living individual of the species *Homo sapiens*. But in the new sense, no: we are speaking of one who has so far attained very little in the way of development or maturity.

So, as by a kind of verbal trick, it becomes possible for some people to deny the humanity of the unborn child *and get away with it*. "But you've just agreed that it isn't a person!"

For the sake of linguistic as well as moral propriety, they shouldn't be allowed to get away with it. As always, let terms be defined.

The whole question of abortion is plagued by verbal falsity, since few people are willing to face the reality of what they're saying: "Why shouldn't we kill our unwanted children? It's often been done in the past, even in highly civilised societies!" Such candour as that is not yet socially acceptable, though we're coming along; so there have to be clouds of non-language, of verbal fog, to which this new ambiguity of 'person' makes a substantial contribution.

Horrors then abound. There are some people who, when attempting to define what's lacked by the unborn child, speak of 'meaningful personhood' (see MEANINGFUL). How can they do it? What has the poor language done to deserve such treatment?

PILGRIM CHURCH, THE

Like 'THE PEOPLE OF GOD', this is a somewhat two-faced expression. It can be used in a fully Catholic sense. But by that very fact, one can easily be distracted from noticing its frequent use in a subtly different sense. That makes it into a useful weapon for those who seek a transformation of our Church-and-Faith into something other than what she is, something preferred by themselves. There are many such people. Their state of conscience, of good or bad faith, is no concern of ours. But we need to beware of what they're saying.

Yes, the Church is rather like a pilgrim, a traveller: she goes journeying down the centuries, keeping her eyes always fixed upon her destination, her ultimate rendezvous with the returning Lord. So it can be innocent—I'm not sure that it's very useful—to speak of 'the Pilgrim Church'.

But that can also be a code-expression for what

some people call 'ongoing revelation'. It isn't so innocent then.

At the best, I see there the operation of a possibly unconscious desire to have theology assimilated to the pattern of the natural sciences. In view of the achievement and prestige of those sciences, that's very understandable. But the two cases are not and cannot be parallel.

For one thing, the scientist possesses a particularly rigorous tool of discovery, the repeatable experiment made under controlled conditions. No theologian, no religious enquirer has access to anything similar. We speak of 'religious EXPERIENCE' —that of the great mystics, for example—but that is not at all the same thing.

Then, the scientist must always hold himself ready to revise or reject earlier thinking in the light of new findings: in principle, his notion of 'truth' is always provisional. But a Catholic, as such, is committed to a very different notion of 'truth'. It's the truth of God, the "Faith once committed to the Saints", and there's nothing provisional about it.

It can and must 'develop', of course, in the sense classically defined by Newman. But that isn't a process of radically new discovery. It can sometimes present a superficial appearance of that sort, as when the Immaculate Conception was defined, or papal infallibility. But those doctrines and others had always been lurking there in the Church's subconscious (if I may put it that way), and they had commonly been enacted for a very long time before getting fully spelled out, often rather late in the day. (We speak of 'the early Church', but it can't all have seemed so very early at the time. When the Council of Ephesus finally got around to spelling out the true humanity of our Lord and the true dignity of our Lady as 'Mother of God', the Incarnation was ancient history: it lay farther off in "the dark backward and abysm of time" than the Spanish Armada lies today.)

The scientist unearths some previously unsuspected truth: the Church apprehends ancient truth in ever-increasing depth and fullness and precision. God does not change his mind.

If that expression 'the Pilgrim Church' suggested only a journey through time to an eschatological destination, it would be harmless enough. But since it is so often used to suggest a quasi-scientific journey *into* truth—as though earlier teachings could simply be rejected on the basis of new knowledge, just as we now reject the idea of a geocentric universe—a prudent Catholic should avoid it, or at least use it with great caution.

When debating this question, I have often asked for specific instances: "Can you name some ancient teaching from which the Pilgrim Church must now emerge?" In my necessarily limited experience, the teaching primarily and most naturally cited is that of *Humanae vitae*.

That's often what's bothering people most of all, even when they appear to be talking about something totally different. See COLLEGIALITY.

POLITICAL LANGUAGE

I am thinking here of such words and dichotomies as 'Liberal' and 'Conservative' or 'Left' and 'Right'. As found in the vocabulary of politics, each carries a heavy emotional loading but is semantically in chaos: each serves mostly as a chosen style in tribal war-paint. Where serious political analysis is attempted—as distinct from tribal conflict—such language throws every real issue into confusion. But that doesn't bother many of us, since hate-filled partisanship is a far more popular activity than accurate thinking.

Between politics and religion, between State and Church, the relationship can vary. The two are hardly distinguished in Islamic societies but are kept rigorously apart—theoretically at least—in the United States. An old tradition tells us that politics is a branch of ethics or morality, which is fine so long as it doesn't lead us to suppose that political activity is normally virtuous; and it does suggest that the two can't really be kept apart.

Every political cause claims to have righteous foundations and likes to have influential backing; and what foundation could be more righteous, what backer more influential, than God? Accordingly, we find many religious people—even good Catholics—claiming religious sanctions for their various political preferences. In my time, I have been told by Catholics that when understood in depth and fully accepted, our Faith *requires* each one of us to be a Monarchist, a believer in aristocracy and the hereditary principle, even a kind of Clerico-Fascist. I have also been told, by other Catholics, that it *requires* us to believe in Liberal Democracy or even in a barely qualified Marxism.

Such delusions are more pathetic in Catholics than in others, since we ought to be well informed about the requirements of belief. We should be able to see that in politics, there's nothing corresponding to Divine Revelation on the one hand or to empirical observation and hard scientific findings on the other. We ought to be political agnostics, intellectually but morally too. If we define 'politics' empirically, as 'the kind of activity that goes on at Westminster and Washington', it turns out to be mostly a matter of people *quarrelling*; and if we follow the Prince of Peace, we should hold aloof from that and from the fictitious certainties by which it gets rationalised.

Our semantic problem—and it's a very serious one—arises when the language of politics is carried over into questions of faith and morals, as when we hear of some 'Conservative' Bishop or some 'Liberal' theologian. I first came across this confusion in the United States, but, to my regret, it has now spread to England. It does any amount of harm: for one thing, it makes many people suppose that fidelity to Catholic tradition entails commitment to the political Right, whereas there are in fact certain points at which the two are sharply in conflict. It can also happen the other way round; and since the Lord speaks in a still small voice while the passions of political partisanship bellow very loudly indeed, the outcome can be extremely sad.

I suggest that if we want to keep our Catholic vocabulary in good working order, we should kick all political and quasi-political terminology right out of it. In faith and morals, the only useful dichotomy is that between the 'orthodox' and the more or less 'heretical'.

RELEVANT

This is one of those incomplete words. Nothing can be 'relevant' in the abstract, in general. Relevant *to what*? That question needs to have some sort of answer, sometimes implied by the context and totally obvious, sometimes needing to be spelled out for the sake of clarity. But it has to be there: otherwise the word means nothing.

There has always been religious controversy. But during my own lifetime, it has undergone a curious shift of emphasis. People used to say that our Catholic Faith wasn't true: now, they are more likely to say that it isn't 'relevant'. They don't care whether it's true or not: they don't see it as something that concerns them at all, one way or the other.

Where something or somebody claims (among other things) to resolve the problem of death, such indifference is a strange thing: after all, death is the one thing that undeniably does concern every single one of us.

But we can see what such people mean. While our Faith is of total relevance to the *real* human condition, it's more or less totally irrelevant to the various fantasy-versions of human existence which are widely preferred to its distinctly painful reality. How do *you* see the main business of life? Do you see it in terms of getting rich and powerful, of retaining unbroken good health, of feeling nicely adjusted and fulfilled, of enjoying 'a high standard of living' and a rewarding social life, with plenty of sexual fun thrown in for seasoning? Well, you may possibly secure some or all of these things. But the Church is totally 'irrelevant' to any such vision of the human condition: she offers you no help at all.

In particular, the Catholic Faith only becomes 'relevant' when you experience guilt and begin to see yourself as a sinner (but see GUILT). C. S. Lewis put it well in *The Problem of Pain* (chapter four): "Christ takes it for granted that men are bad. Until we really feel this assumption of His to be true, though we are part of the world He came to save, we are not part of the audience to whom His words are addressed. We lack the first condition for understanding what He is talking about." And in our time, of course, the sense of personal guilt has become enormously weakened, so that few people are aware of needing forgiveness and redemption more than they need anything else. They lack "ears to hear", and the Lord's words and work lack all 'relevance' to what they perceive as their condition.

This word can, of course, be used in less sweeping senses. A Catholic might attribute total 'relevance' to the Faith as such, while denying it to certain details of Catholic practice. It might be argued that certain Counter-Reformation styles of devotion, having been developed in a psychological and cultural climate very unlike our own, have ceased to be spiritually helpful and (in that sense) 'relevant'.

But in my view, this is a word that we should use with great precision or not at all. It's a *damaged* word, having been overused in the most unthinking manner for many years: like MEANINGFUL, it has become a jargon-word of the emptiest sort, vaguely positive by implication but carrying no specific meaning at all.

As so misused, it has become something of a joke. I'm glad to see that a good many of us, when seeking to parody the more flatulent nonthought of the last two decades or so, naturally speak of something-or-other as being both 'meaningful' and 'relevant'.

When you speak in that satirical manner, be sure to make the quotation marks clearly audible.

RENEWAL

An optimistic word: it suggests springtime. Some optimistic Catholics like to speak of 'the great postconciliar renewal'. That illustrates the tremendous power of blind faith.

Here as always, let us attend to ambiguity. 'Renewal' can mean two very different things.

Let us imagine that I have a shabby old tweed jacket, as in fact I have. It's in a terrible state, it needs renewal. So I patch the cuffs and the elbows, I sew the buttons on again, I repair the ruptured pockets, I wipe off the worst of the beer-stains, and then I have the whole thing cleaned. Renewal! It looks . . . well, not quite as it looked in its first virginity, but much better than it did.

That's one sort of 'renewal'. But at some stage, I may decide to rob a bank and 'renew' my entire wardrobe. That means that I shall sling the whole lot out and buy new garments, far better, far more suited to my dignity (but see DIGNITY).

Not the same thing. 'Renewal' can be a matter

of restoring or a matter of replacing.

If we attend carefully to the doings of the Second Vatican Council, and to the words of Pope John XXIII that preceded it and defined the object of the exercise, we shall find that the 'renewal' there intended was of the first kind. Not that the preconciliar Church bore any close resemblance to my disgusting old jacket. But she was a pretty fair shambles, like anything else that has human beings in it; and so it was when the Council of Trent was summoned and earlier. *Ecclesia semper reformanda* has never been a new discovery or a passing phase: just like you and me, the Church has always needed to pull her socks up, to work upon her own incessant failure.

But some people talk as though 'postconciliar renewal' meant not a repair but a replacement of the old Church, the old Faith, and by something radically different: not old garments repaired but new garments bought from elsewhere, even a new identity. Remember the difference, whenever you hear this springtime word invoked.

The great mistake of some people was that of supposing that there could be a renewal or resurrection without a preceding death, an Easter Sunday without a preceding Good Friday. The Lord's different view is foreshadowed throughout all mythology, all comparative religion: *Nisi granum frumenti*. . . .

SACRIFICE

This is an important word for Catholics, if only because the sacrificial nature of the Mass is being doubted or denied by many and needs stout reassertion. But what shall we be saying when we reassert it? What *is* sacrifice?

The trouble is that in common usage, this word has lost one-half of its ancient meaning. It now suggests little more than self-denial. "My boy, your mother and I made great sacrifices to put you through college": that is to say, they went without certain luxuries.

Now from its very ancient beginnings, the concept of 'sacrifice' did include that element of renunciation or self-denial. There had to be a victim, not necessarily animate: it might be a bird or an animal or even a man, but it might also be a quantity of corn or oil or wine or incense. But whatever it might be, it wasn't there when the sacrifice was over; and since it had to be something or somebody of value, that was a self-inflicted deprivation for those concerned. A sacrifice is thus an asceticism.

But it was always much more than that; and the practical difficulty is that when we consider the further meanings of 'sacrifice', we shall need to explore territory which is not only unfamiliar but also uncongenial to characteristically modern people. The psychologist, the anthropologist and the student of comparative religion will know a good deal about that territory. But they will usually have visited it as foreigners, without ever knowing it from the inside.

Consider one obvious example, the story of Abraham and Isaac. It strikes us as meaningless barbarity, even as lunacy. In what state of mind would a father be if he deemed it his religious duty to murder his own son? And what kind of God could possibly order him to do so, with or without any last-minute change of mind? And yet Catholic tradition requires us to see all that as neither barbaric nor insane, but as a most sacred prefiguring of another Father and another Son, with a different kind of wood being carried up the sacrificial mountain.

But what then? Many a virtuous man has been tortured to death unjustly: can we really see the Crucifixion as anything more than another meaningless abomination? How can it possibly have modified the entire human condition, and very much for the better? Every Catholic child will say that "Christ died for our sins" and will speak of his 'sacrifice' on the Cross and therefore at Mass: let's hope that he clings to that faith. But in these days, isn't it rather a *blind* faith? Does such language correspond to anything in his mental world?

Many a tribal primitive would have got the message at once: he'd have seen the point.

For most of us and to our loss, the whole concept of sacrifice—of worship and redemption by blood—has become simply opaque. We're too civilised for it, too refined: we try to use that word 'sacrifice', but we find that it's died on us.

H. G. Wells once described the Mass as a barbarian blood-feast, which made Chesterton very angry indeed. But for all the narrow vulgarity of his mind, Wells was there closer to the mark than those who now reduce it into a social occasion of cheerful togetherness and uplift.

Unlike some, ours is a religion of blood-sacrifice. The Catholic mind—when at its deepest—has far more in common with the primitive and pagan mind than either has in common with the humanitarian and positivistic mind which dominates most present-day society. Not long ago, in the days of confidently asserted white superiority, that would have seemed a very damaging confession. It shouldn't look like that today.

SCHISM

Like that other six-letter word HERESY, this has become something of a dirty word, but only when invoked in connection with present-day separations. You may still use it with reference to the distant past: no cheek will blush if you mention the Photian 'schism', and certain Catholics—of a self-castigating type that abounds today—will positively rejoice if you harp sardonically upon the 'Great Schism'. On the other hand, you mustn't say that specified individuals and groups of today are 'in schism' while others are not. That would be unecumenical and therefore offensive.

Even so, this isn't quite such a dirty word as 'heresy', since it isn't so inherently unsymmetrical. It can allow for a certain mutuality, a sharing of blame for what all recognise as a deplorable situation. 'Heresy' must always carry a suggestion of "We're right and you're wrong." 'Schism' can do so as well, but not necessarily: it can suggest "We are estranged, and that's very unfortunate; but who can say whether it's more our fault or yours?"

Where there's any sort of estrangement, it's our natural human instinct to say "It was all your fault!" Charity and humility will rightly dispose a Christian to say something different: "It may have been our fault quite as much, or even more." Readiness to say that is a very laudable thing.

But let us be careful. Charity and humility are high virtues. But *corruptio optimi pessima*, "Lilies that fester smell far worse than weeds." It's obviously unpleasant to climb down and accept the blame. But for some people, it can be even more unpleasant to stand by, in apparent complacency, while the other party climbs down and accepts the blame. Pride can then be involved—the pride of displayed humility.

Estrangement or 'schism' isn't always symmetrical, and truth matters no less than charity.

The word comes, as does 'scissors', from a root which means 'to cut'. So does 'insect', since those little creatures appear to be nearly cut in half: 'sect', however, comes from 'to follow'—an associated meaning but a different root.

The practical question is whether the 'schism' or cutting-off of Christians is always symmetrical. There was once a book of joke-history, a very amusing parody, called *1066 and All That*; and it said of the English Reformation that "the Pope and all his followers then seceded from the Church of England." Well, you *can* put it that way round.

But . . . see UNITY, CHRISTIAN.

SERVE

You 'serve' anybody when you do such things for him, at his express or implied request, as were once done for him by his *servus* or slave or serf or servant. We don't have slaves or serfs nowadays, and few of us have domestic servants. But it's still a prime duty to serve others.

The central concept here is that of *obedience*, a word which has become so very unfashionable in some Catholic circles as to have practically disappeared from sight. No doubt we always practised that virtue very imperfectly. But it's a new and alarming situation when we forget that it *is* a virtue—that *Non serviam* ("I refuse to obey") was always the motto of Hell (see AUTHORITY).

The element of obedience is obvious enough where orders or commands are given, as by a master to his servant or by the High Command to a serving officer. But it's still present, in a slightly different version, where we 'serve' others on some wholly voluntary basis of pure charity. We still have to act in conformity to what they desire, or would desire if they had considered the matter, and might well command if that were on the cards. A 'service' inflicted upon some reluctant victim is no real 'service' at all. (We can allow for certain exceptions here. A doctor or dentist will sometimes do most beneficial 'service' to a frightened and struggling child.)

So far, so good. The trouble begins when we say (as some of us do) that the Church exists in order to 'serve' the WORLD.

There's a clear sense in which she does. She exists to 'serve' the Lord above all else, and she does so—partly, not wholly—by doing the best of all possible 'services' to fallen and despairing mankind. But she doesn't (or shouldn't) 'serve' the world in any sense of taking orders from it and obeying them punctiliously. Her orders come from above.

If we forget this, we can easily fall into a very ancient mistake, one that appears to have been made by the Lord's disciples. I think of them scratching their heads in perplexity and saying, "But Rabbi, how will *that* help us to kick the bloody Romans out and reestablish the Kingdom of Israel?" And I think of the Lord as replying—in his truly divine immunity to impatience and irritation—"But I wasn't *talking* about that sort of thing! I didn't come in order to solve the world's problems, as seen by itself and on its own terms! My Kingdom is of an altogether different sort!"

One trouble with the world—that is, with natural or unredeemed humanity—is that it doesn't really know what it wants: the true Object of human desire lies beyond human experience. So if the Church were to 'serve' it—in the sense of taking its orders and so attempting to solve what it sees as its problems—the consequences would be falsity and frustration and failure at the best, a kind of Hell at the worst.

If you want to know what the world sees as its problems, turn to any newspaper. They've been around for a long time, they don't change much. But the Church has also been around for a long time; and I don't think it's so very shocking to say that when it comes to 'serving the world' by solving its own problems on its own terms, the Church doesn't appear to be a very effective instrument. I would like to believe that the old Papal States were models of perfect government; but they weren't. The Church isn't *for* that kind of thing. Her success is mostly invisible: we glimpse it microscopically at every canonisation.

Many of us now *want* the Church to 'serve' the

world in the sense of taking its orders. But as they seem to realise, that requires us to cook up something totally different and agree to call it 'the Church'. That won't be very honest, and it certainly won't work.

See RELEVANT.

SIN

There was once an elderly man to whom the pastor delicately mentioned this subject of sin. He laughed. "*Sin*, Father? That doesn't bother me any more: hell, I'm in my sixties!"

He had forgotten that there are seven Deadly Sins, not just one.

This concept is absolutely necessary to any Catholic apostolate, since no Redeemer could be RELEVANT if we weren't sinners. But, semantically speaking, the word is now in poor shape and an obstacle to easy communication. Along with various related words, it carries those overwhelmingly sexual overtones in practically every context, even where no such particular emphasis is intended. 'Losing one's virtue', 'an immoral woman', 'living in sin': if any such expression turned out to have no sexual reference at all, it would almost be seen as a kind of pun. And yet one can be desperately wicked while totally chaste.

We can hardly discard this crucial word 'sin', but we can at least prevent such misunderstandings by explanation and also by surrounding and alternating it with synonyms, of which 'wickedness' might well be one. Terms which suggest 'breaking the rules' are usually best avoided: where possible, a hint of 'betraying one's best Friend' can be helpful.

The expression 'original sin' creates further difficulties—partly because it so easily gives a suggestion that a newborn baby can be personally guilty of great wickedness, and partly because it sidetracks many minds into questions of Old Testament exegesis and hermeneutics. Here as elsewhere, a translation into modern jargon can prove useful: "a hereditary estrangement from the Ground of our own being" can be a good start, since it indicates a sad fact of universal experience, lamented by the poets. But we can't stop there, of course.

Within our fully traditional Catholic vocabulary, this word 'sin' has a further weakness, heightened by the confessor's practice of asking us *how often* we have committed the sin in question. This gave the word an excessively *digital* emphasis. When I'm asked how many people I've murdered or how many young ladies I've seduced, I always find it possible to give a statistically precise answer:

such deeds are distinct from one another and are easily remembered. But where 'sin' lies—hardly less seriously—in some sustained habit of thought and word and minor deed, figures are unlikely to be available and would matter little if they were.

It's sometimes more realistic to speak of chronic 'sinfulness' or 'wickedness' than of distinct 'sins' —that is, so long as the offence is not thereby palliated.

SOCIAL and SOCIALISM

These words have entirely respectable antecedents. The Latin word *socius* means 'companion': in formal documents, it is still applied to the 'fellows' of an Oxford or Cambridge college, as distinct from such comparable scholars as live and work alone. In its later derivatives, it often carried a note of alliance or confederacy.

In current usage, 'social' can be a simple antonym of 'individual'; and since excessive individualism can be a matter of self-love at the expense of others, we ought to be perfectly happy with such expressions as 'the social gospel'. There are two Great Commandments, not just the first.

But in practice, we cannot be altogether happy and off our guard where this word is concerned. It has recently undergone a certain semantic pollution, and so has a tendency to poison every sentence into which it makes its way. If a man calls out for 'justice', we should listen carefully: he or others may be suffering some real injustice that needs to be rectified. But if he calls out for 'social justice', be on your guard: he's selling you some ideological package of the most questionable sort. And if you display any sales-resistance, you can inadvertently allow yourself to seem like one who favours injustice.

When thus polluted, this word 'social' becomes a useful instrument of verbal trickery, even of verbal blackmail. It needs watching.

The related words 'socialism' and 'socialist' came into the English language in the early nineteenth century. In each, the central idea is that of economic resources and activities being controlled by the community, not by the individual. But by *what* community? By the State, the government? That's taken for granted in present-day usage, and most of us speak of 'socialism' where a purist would prefer to speak of 'State socialism'. But in the earlier usage of Robert Owen and others, the community which controlled the economic resources and activities was to be the small and local community of those who actually did the work in question. In this sense, 'socialism' is Chesterton's 'Distributism', as extended to activities that are too large and complex for one man to handle on his own.

But in this sense, the word is practically obsolete;

so in order to avoid cross-purposes, it's better to speak of 'worker-ownership' or 'the cooperative ideal'. Among economic ideals, this has the surely unique distinction of having been warmly praised by both Ronald Reagan and Leonid Brezhnev. It is also in close harmony with the mind of the Church.

But that doesn't cover the entire semantic complexity of this word 'socialism'. There are European languages in which its local version carries a primary sense of 'institutionalised atheism' or 'the anticlerical State'. So if you find some Pope condemning 'socialism' by name, as Pius XI did in *Quadragesimo anno*, you mustn't infer that he was proposing untrammeled free-enterprise capitalism as a suitable ideal for Catholics.

ULTRAMONTANISM

Ambiguity exists within many a word, even sharp semantic tension, even something close to contradiction. But flat *reversal* of effective meaning is a rare thing. This word is a case in point.

Etymologically, those people are 'ultramontane' who live on the other side of the mountains—of the Alps in this case. But which is the 'other' side? That depends on where you're standing.

On its first appearance, this adjective was understood as being applied *by* Italians *to* Frenchmen: Bacon and other sixteenth-century writers use it in that sense. France is traditionally called "the eldest daughter of the Church", and eldest daughters may well be troublemakers, as this one has often been: we extend the word 'Gallican' to cover any national or local desire to play down the papal primacy into something purely nominal (see also COLLEGIALITY). That's a widespread and partly political desire—I hear rumours of it from present-

ULTRAMONTANISM

day America—and it's what was first meant by 'ultramontanism'.

But by the eighteenth century, the word had turned itself completely around: then—and up to the present time—it was understood as being applied *by* Frenchmen *to* Italians. More generally, it now indicates a desire to exalt the papal primacy, and to a degree that has sometimes been rather preposterous. Some English converts, overreacting from their Protestant background, spoke as though every utterance of every Pope were automatically infallible in the fullest sense. Such a belief, when historically considered, proves self-contradictory at a number of points.

It was also condemned, in effect, by the First Vatican Council, whose definition of papal infallibility was so restrictive as to constitute a real disappointment for ultramontane opinion.

The older sense of this word is now so completely forgotten as to generate no serious danger of misunderstanding. But we still need to be careful, since it is often applied—strictly as a smear-word—to those who question the self-conferred infallibility of the 'progressive' or 'liberal' Catholic intelligentsia.

Such an energumen once applied it to myself. "What on earth do you mean?", I asked. By way of reply, he seized a dictionary and pointed with quivering finger at what it said: an ultramontane was one who held exaggerated ideas about the papal office.

"But 'exaggerated' by what standard?" You can't describe any ideas as being 'exaggerated' without reference to some notion of what would be more appropriate, more balanced and realistic.

But my friend had no such notion. He simply hated the papacy.

'Ultramontanism', like many another word, cannot be taken at its face value when on the lips of the frenzied.

UNITY, CHRISTIAN

This expression is used in two distinct ways.

a. It can refer to something that once did exist, was then shattered and now needs repairing—by friendly togetherness at the grass-roots level (see ECUMENISM) and also by quasi-political negotiations at the ecclesiastical summit.

b. It can refer to something which existed unbrokenly from the start and still does exist, but with which many groups and individuals have got into a bad relationship. It thus calls for a return rather than for any sort of repair.

In the first of these two senses, the expression 'Christian unity' seems to me entirely phantasmal. Did it ever really exist? At the precise moment of the first Pentecost, doubtlessly. But in this sense of the word, the New Testament shows us a Church that was already divided, not only at Corinth; and so it continues in the later story, right up to the present day. For controversial reasons, some people like to invoke the vision and model of 'the undivided early Church'. But that's a myth.

Then, while friendly togetherness is an excellent thing, it doesn't cause real questions to go away or resolve themselves by magic. But it does encourage people to brush them aside as endangering friendship. The cause of 'Christian unity', as so understood and so pursued, thus does something without precedent in Christian history: it causes doctrine to be treated as secondary and unimportant, so promoting relativism and indeed an effective agnosticism.

Then, how are we to see negotiation—with goodwill all round, with compromise where necessary, with much give-and-take—as a road to 'Christian unity'? That's an admirable and necessary method where there's only a conflict of *interest*: it's how two countries manage to sign a treaty, it's how lawsuits are sometimes settled out of court. But it makes no sense at all where any question of possible *truth* is involved. "I'm sure that with patience and goodwill, we'll be able to hit on a formula that will prove acceptable on all sides": can you imagine somebody attempting to resolve a scientific or scholarly dispute on those lines?

Once again, that first understanding of 'Christian unity' assumes and also promotes doctrinal relativism and an effective agnosticism. Its popularity appears to stem from a good-natured but arbitrary assumption that Christian *dis*unity, as now existing, has got to be symmetrical, with no more blame carried there than here.

Throughout the New Testament, by sharp contrast, unity is treated as a datum of marked particularity. If you departed from it, you unchurched yourself. That's the Catholic understanding of 'Christian unity', and the only understanding that makes real sense unless CHRISTIANITY is to be reduced to benevolent togetherness and altruism alone.

In the last theological analysis, that expression can only be a name of Christ; and is Christ divided? God forbid. But he can always be abandoned—more or less totally, more or less permanently. A penitent return is then the only proper thing—morally, spiritually, personally and ecclesiastically as well.

VALID

This word comes from a Latin verb meaning 'to be in good health'. A chronically sick person can still be called an 'invalid'.

If you're 'valid' or healthy, you should be able to perform more or less effectively; and with that sort of emphasis, the word came into the English language as a primarily legal term, seldom or never with any sort of medical implication. A licence or permit, say, is 'valid' or effective up to a certain date, and under the provisions of a statute or something similar: the old medical sense is echoed in the fact that it then 'expires', like an unfortunate invalid. Americans often use 'effective' in this chiefly legal sense, and also—as at the heart of your airline ticket—'good'.

That's the primary sense in which 'valid' drifted over into Canon Law and so into the Catholic vocabulary in general. But its meaning there has been complicated by a separate sense of 'reality'.

In certain circumstances, for example, a sacramental act can be 'valid but illicit'. That excommunicated bishop had no canonical right to ordain you, but he did, and you really are a priest in the sight of God. In the same way, an 'invalid' marriage is no marriage at all.

Any careless use of 'valid' therefore invites confusion between authorised effectiveness—legal or canonical—and objective reality.

Much confusion of that sort has arisen in connection with the possible 'validity' of Anglican orders. Leo XIII used clearer and more resonant language: in 1896, he declared them to be "absolutely null and utterly void"—to lack all reality, that is. Many Catholics prefer to speak more gently and to deny, or sometimes to assert, their 'validity'.

But the legal or legalistic past of that word then suggests that the Pope was giving a judgment of the juridical or administrative sort, such as might be reversed at any time by the relevant authority, as when an expired licence is given new validity by statute. He was actually giving his judgment on a point of fact, and you can't alter facts by statute.

This confusion pervades what they call the 'ecumenical dialogue', especially as between Rome and Canterbury. Time and time again, we there see 'mutual recognition of ministries' proposed as one step toward the rainbow's end of 'reunion', and very much as two nations might grant diplomatic recognition to one another by juridical or administrative acts of some appropriate sort.

That's a pleasingly eirenical proposal, of course; and it's always unpleasant to say to some good man "You are not really what you appear and claim to be." But that's no worse than when a doctor needs to say "You are not really as healthy as you appear and suppose."

Unless Catholic sacramental theology has been misguided from the start, priesthood—like Christian MARRIAGE—is quite as objective as a tumour. We do our best to find out whether it's there or not, and the ambiguity of 'valid' doesn't help. 'Real' is often a better word.

In recent years, 'valid' has taken on a new lease of quasi-life as a meaningless junk-word (see MEANINGFUL). It then indicates nothing more than vaguely defensive approval, as when sodomy is said to be "a valid life-style".

When I am dictator, my Linguistic Police will pounce most fiercely on all such perversions—of the language, that is.

WAR

Saint Thomas says somewhere that it's better to live in the city than in the country. That's one in the eye for those Catholics—I am one of them—who prefer rural life and are possibly guilty of romantic agrarianism.

But when Saint Thomas delivered that judgment, he naturally had in mind the cities of his own time; and those were very small by our standards, hardly isolated at all from 'Nature' and the life of the surrounding countryside. Many of them would seem to us like small towns rather than 'cities'. I suspect that if Saint Thomas had been given a prophetic glimpse of present-day London or New York, he would have supposed himself to be beholding a vision of Hell.

My point is that a word can retain its old dictionary definition while referring to some vastly altered reality.

As with 'city', so with 'war'. A solid moral

tradition assures us that 'the just war' is at least a theoretical possibility: it isn't a contradiction in terms, as the pacifists maintain. In order to be 'just', of course, it has to satisfy certain conditions, such as are seldom satisfied—and hardly ever *recognisably* satisfied—in any concrete historical situation.

But it isn't always the same kind of thing. That word 'war' retains its old dictionary definition. But thanks to technological development and the power of national and ideological passion, it can now refer to a reality utterly unlike what our Catholic forefathers had in mind when they spoke of 'war' and found it very occasionally justifiable.

Things said truly about swords and spears will not necessarily be said truly about instruments of indiscriminate mass destruction. So this word needs careful watching, especially when we apply ancient judgments to modern circumstances.

WORLD

This word plays a rather curious part in our Catholic vocabulary, partly because of its built-in ambiguity. Is the 'world' a good thing? Yes: God loved it into existence, and so much that he sent his only Son for its redemption. But it's also an enemy which the Lord claimed to have defeated: it has Satan for its Prince, and along with the Flesh and the Devil, it's something that we have to renounce.

Perhaps we should have two separate words for it. In the former and positive sense, we can speak of the *kosmos* in Greek and the *mundus* in Latin: in the latter and negative sense, we can say *aion* or *saeculum* with reference to a place and period of exceptionally evil character, due to be replaced by something much better.

A place *and* period? In this age, we instinctively regard space and time as utterly distinct and unrelated. Our forefathers did not always do so, however; and unless I am grossly mistaken, Einstein implied that their instinct may have been sounder than our own. In English, 'world' itself comes from two Anglo-Saxon words which add up the 'life-span of humanity': it was about time rather than space to begin with, and, in our older literature, you can find it used with either emphasis or with both together.

In recent Catholic usage, the word was often contrasted sharply with the technically 'religious' life of the monastery or convent. Certain nuns—more inward-looking, perhaps, than was altogether healthy—would speak as though those Catholics who lived 'in the world' added up to an eccentric and slightly reprehensible minority.

But the pendulum has swung sharply, and even a mildly negative use of the word is uncommon today. Its dominant sense is positive to the point of enthusiasm. For many of us, 'OPENNESS to the world' and 'involvement in the world' are virtues which the Church now practises better than she did though still insufficiently.

That makes a kind of sense. It's clearly a bad thing for Catholics to remain simply ignorant of current fashions in secular or 'worldly' thought: we can't all be monks or hermits, and the love of one's neighbour requires concern for his temporal well-being, not only for his salvation. Beyond that, unguarded negativism about 'the world' might easily foster a kind of Manichaeanism, as though this lovely planet were hateful and the work of some demiurge or devil.

But unguarded positivism about it suggests something equally dangerous—a quasi-Pelagian optimism about this *aion* or *saeculum* of ours, as though there were nothing wrong with the world which couldn't be put to rights by sufficient effort and know-how and dedication. (The American mind is particularly prone to this sort of Utopianism, at least so far as the American 'world' is concerned.)

The trouble is, of course, a sharply weakened sense of original sin—which has to be seen, in some mysterious way, as affecting the nonhuman creation as well as ourselves. We're a damaged species, we live in a damaged world, and even the best human society will be built out of flawed materials. It follows that all temporal optimism has to be cautious and qualified.

The darker sense of 'world' needs a certain reemphasis. It seems to be mostly forgotten. When did you last hear a sermon about the sin of 'worldliness'?

EPILOGUE

Although set forth alphabetically, this is not a work of reference. I offer it as an essay, intended to draw attention to a certain range of practical problems, mostly stemming from ambiguity: only in the most limited and tentative manner do I attempt their resolution.

I conclude with a twofold warning, already foreshadowed in my Introduction.

We are Catholic apostles, preaching the Word—crucially though not exclusively—by means of words. But if our choice of those words is limited to the real vernacular of a secular culture, while something will get across, it won't be our sacred *Logos*. This may be why so many of us prefer to concentrate upon temporal welfare and social justice and similar questions, since "communication" there seems so much easier. But "communication" of *what*?

At the other extreme, some of us confine ourselves to the conceptual and verbal systems of Catholic tradition. The danger then is that our sacred *Logos*, while rightly honoured, will fail to get across. Here are two minor instances. If we talk as though "peace" meant "the tranquility of order" and as though "law" meant "an ordinance of reason for the common good", we shall simply bewilder those people—and they are the vast majority—in whose *de facto* vocabulary each word indicates something very different.

So with even weightier matters. The burdensome fact is that we need to be sensitively bilingual. But that was always one of the most daunting tasks that faced the missionary.

November 7, 1986   C. H. D.